This book is your child's ticket
off the emotional rollercoaster.
Take a deep breath
and enjoy the new ride.

For information about this title or to order other books
and/or electronic media, contact the publisher:

Mindful Aromatherapy, LLC
www.MindfulAromatherapy.com
MindfulAromatherapy@gmail.com

Library of Congress Control Number: 2015914086
ISBN: 978-0-9966585-0-8

Printed in the United States of America

Cover and Interior design: 1106 Design
Edited by Jeannine E. Patel, M.A. Ed
Illustrated by Stacy Heller Budnick

Publisher's Cataloging-In-Publication Data on file

How to get your child excited about chilling out . . .

When reading *Mad to Glad* aloud, encourage children to act out the instructions associated to each emotion. Read the stories often, and practice daily.

Mindfulness is paying attention to the present moment in a non-judgemental way. This mindful awareness stops our brains from pondering the "I should haves" of yesterday and worrying about the "What ifs?" of tomorrow.

In my experience with teaching Mindfulness to children, I realized emotions, both positive and negative, require awareness. I wrote this short story to help children become aware of common reactions to everyday situations. This book helps children recognize their emotions while they are experiencing the emotion. With guidance and practice, this internal awareness enables the child to create space between the challenging experience and their emotional and physical reaction.

My mission is to help children recognize that anger, frustration, sadness, and loneliness are common emotions, and it is natural to feel them every now and then. This book contains simple exercises, inspired by my own Mindfulness practice, to help children increase their coping abilities. Your child will learn to transfer their energy from fear and anger into positive thoughts and actions that serve their social and emotional growth.

Written for ages 3–7

I am happy. I am good.
Well, most of the time

I Feel Happy.

My mom says

I Am Good

all of the time.

She says even when I make bad choices

I Am Always Good.

But what about when other people make choices that affect me?

Do you want
to know
something?

When other people
make choices
that affect me,
I feel . . .

Mad!

I am so mad!

My little brother **took** my ball.

Mom said I have to **share** my stuff
with him because
that is how he learns
to share.

I feel since I am older,
I am the only one
who has to share.

It does not feel fair!

Mom said I can

jump up
and down

until the

mad

goes away.

Can you try
jumping up and down
ten times?

9

How do you feel
after you jump up
and down ten times?

I feel better.
I can jump really,
really high!

10

Repeat with me out loud:

When other people make choices
that affect me, I feel . . .

Frustrated!

I am frustrated!

I saw Lila on the monkey bars today and she
went all the way across to the other side
by herself!

I have tried the monkey bars so many times and
I cannot make it more than two or three bars.

Will I ever be able to make it all the way across
the monkey bars?

Tonight, I am going to ask the stars out my window to send me a special dream. In my dream, I can go all the way across the monkey bars!

I feel the bars in my hands as I swing from
bar to bar until I am safe at the other end!

15

Can you

close your eyes

and

feel

the bars in your hands, and

imagine

your body swinging
from bar to bar?

Feel how

happy

you are to make it all the way
across the monkey bars.

Repeat with me out loud:

When other people make choices
that affect me, I feel . . .

Sad!

I am so sad.

I asked for a new toy today and
my parents said,

"No!"

My big sister said that when I
feel sad,
I should think about my happiest time ever.

I feel
happiest
when I swing really high on the swing at
the park.

Last week, I was so high my feet almost
touched the sky, and I swung so fast my
hair moved when the wind hit my face.

It was
great!

What is your happiest time ever?

Repeat with me out loud:

When other people
make choices
that affect me,
I feel . . .

Fear.

I feel

afraid!

Mom and Dad said
it is time for bed.
I sleep in
my big bed,
in my own room,
all by myself.

I like my room
in the daytime,
but at night I

hear noises.

It is so dark in here.
I feel

afraid.

25

Nana said when I feel

afraid

I can go over all the people who

love me

in my mind.
She taught me how to say the
"May I Be Loved" list.

My list sounds like this . . .

"Mommy loves me.
Daddy loves me.
Nana loves me.
My dog loves me.
The trees love me,"
and so on and so on.

The list is so long of all the people
and animals that love me!
I bet your list is long like mine.

Who loves you?

Nana said that love is the strongest and
bravest thing in the whole world.
She said I have so much love right in my heart.

When I remember to feel loved, I won't be afraid of
anything anymore.

I am safe.
I am loved.

Repeat with me out loud:

When other people
make choices
that affect me, I feel . . .

Lonely.

I feel left out.

I have a very best friend at school.
We have so much fun together.
We went to the park today.
At the park, we saw a boy
who lives next door to my best friend.
We all played together,
except they were leaving me out of
their secret neighborhood games.
I had to play all by myself.

Pop called the feeling,
"lonely."

Pop said whenever I feel

lonely

I can

breathe in

through my nose
really deeply and
blow all the air out
through my mouth.

You try it.
First with your
eyes open, then
try it with your
eyes closed.

Breathe in really big through your nose. Hold it, then
blow it out through your mouth, loud like the wind.

Imagine you are blowing all the lonely feelings
out through your mouth.

It took
five breaths

to make the lonely feeling go away.

My best friend and I play superheroes at school. Maybe his neighbor likes to play superheroes too. I will ask him next time I see him at the park.

33

Repeat with me out loud:

I Am Mindful Diary

Name   Date

_____   _____

_____   _____

_____   _____

_____   _____

_____   _____

_____   _____

_____   _____

_____   _____

_____   _____

_____   _____

_____   _____

_____   _____

_____   _____

The
Happy
Ending

About the Author

Angie Harris is a mother to two brilliant boys and aunt to eight beautiful nieces and nephews. As a teenager Angie suffered the sudden loss of her beloved mother, Rosemarie. It was then she was introduced to contemplative practices such as yoga and meditation. On September 11, 2001 Angie went to work in downtown NYC to witness the horror and tragedy of the attacks on the Twin Towers. Once again she called upon her formal meditation practice to help cope and heal from the trauma. She quickly realized the more she practiced, the more comfort she felt, even while grieving such catastrophic losses.

A decade later, Angie's sister Stephy was diagnosed with cancer. Stephy fought bravely, but lost her battle in 2014. It was at this time that Angie's meditation practice turned outward, toward teaching. She wanted to share meditation with her young nieces and nephews, who are grieving the loss of their mother, as she was once taught to do. To learn how to deliver lessons effectively to children, Angie attended the Mindful Schools K–12 curriculum training in 2012. She is honored to share meditation with students, corporations, and individuals looking to increase their natural coping abilities.

She loves being outdoors with her husband Toby and their two boys, Kellen and Kieren. To learn more or to contact Angie directly, visit *www.MindfulAromatherapy.com*

CPSIA information can be obtained at www.ICGtesting.com
Printed in the USA
BVOW10s1132200915

418702BV00001B/1/P